A Gift For:

Kayla

From:

Grams, Dad, Nicci & Shelby

Copyright © 2012 by Dodinsky
Sourcebooks and the colophon are registered trademarks
of Sourcebooks, Inc.

This edition published in 2014 by Hallmark Gift Books,
a division of Hallmark Cards, Inc., Kansas City, MO 64141
under license from Sourcebooks, Inc.
Visit us on the Web at Hallmark.com.

All rights reserved. No part of this publication may be reproduced,
transmitted, or stored in any form or by any means without the prior
written permission of the publisher.

All brand names and product names used in this book are trademarks,
registered trademarks, or trade names of their respective holders.
Sourcebooks, Inc., is not associated with any product or vendor
in this book.

ISBN: 978-1-59530-742-2
BOK2181

Made in China.
JAN16

SEIZE
YOUR DREAMS

INSPIRATIONS TO FOLLOW YOUR HEART

BY DODINSKY

When you are looking at a mountain, marveling at its beauty and strength, realize it is looking right back and admiring you.

EMBRACE YOUR OWN GREATNESS.

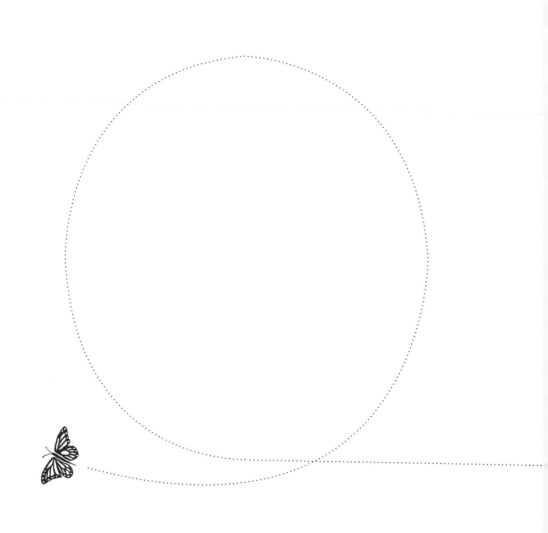

Consider your

HEART

a cocoon from which dreams emerge

like butterflies to

WANDER

in the garden.

Unbind
your spirit.

Don't let
the opinion
of others
restrain you.

I survived my insecurities and though the road is daunting, I have learned being true to oneself is good company.

This one's for you my
beautiful and sweet Kayla ma
you always keep your sl

IF OTHERS WANT TO DEFINE YOU, DON'T LINGER IN THEIR POND.

of wonder and Moana spirit! With much love to you always your Grams (your Grandma Tala ☺)

SWIM AWAY FROM THEIR IGNORANCE AND FIND YOUR OCEAN.

Even if you find your

VOICE,

sometimes it does not matter anymore,

when you speak to someone who is

DEAF

by choice.

I hope when you count the stars, you begin with yourself.

May you embrace the moonlight with your dreams.

The horizon,

to remind
you of your courage,
sends its gentle waves
of confidence to
kiss your feet.

Do not let your shadow walk you.

You are not a slave of the past.

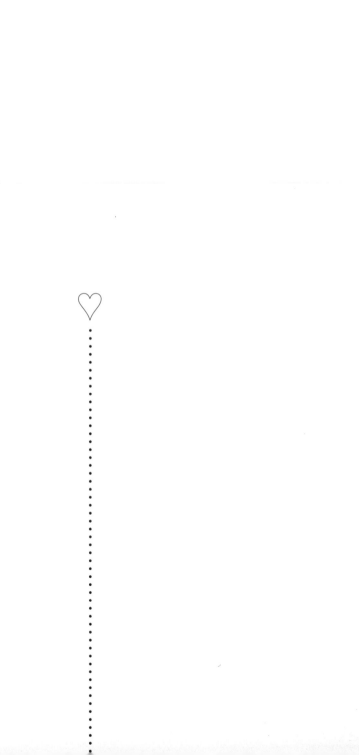

When you go
after your dreams,
sometimes the crowd
yells its wishful thinking.
Ignore that explosion
of opinion, and follow
the trail leading
to your heart.

It will always whisper your truth.

Be there for others, but never leave yourself behind.

THE STRENGTH OF YOUR WILL CANNOT BE IMPRISONED BY OTHER PEOPLE'S IGNORANCE.

Do not become a stranger to yourself
by blending in with everyone else.
Your road to

HAPPINESS

should be

MEMORABLE

for the scenery as well as the destination.

When you stray away from your

SOUL,

the distance you have traveled is
measured by the aching of your

HEART.

If you stumbled today,
remember where and how it felt.
Tomorrow, take a different path.

LIFE

flourishes from its pain and the lessons we gain.

When it seems that
everything you do
is wrong and everyone
is against you—it is
the best time to
wear your

"I don't give a damn" tutu.

Glide gleefully on the dance floor of

"this is me and my life."

If someone you trusted betrayed you **by choice**, don't cuddle up to the rejection or blame yourself.

Why don't you pick yourself up and love yourself better?
This, too, is by choice.

There is a place called happiness; it is just an arm's length away from your fears and a few steps beyond your misgivings. To get there, sometimes you need to take the path of courage down to the street of never-give-up, until you reach the field of dreams.

The question is not why they don't like you
when you are being you.
It is why you waste time
worrying what they think.

If you are not hurting anyone with your

ACTIONS,

keep moving forward with your

LIFE.

EVERY MORNING I START WITH A DRINK FROM MY CUP OF SUNSHINE TO REMIND MYSELF OF WHO I AM BEFORE I STEP INTO THE WORLD OF

"THIS IS WHO WE THINK YOU ARE."

No matter how far
the distance you have
traveled or the failures
that have gathered, hope
would still meet you
anywhere.

It is time to go and leave the past behind.
Exile the thoughts of painful memories.

You have learned what they have taught you.

I hope you see
the luster in the
simplest of things
and heed the
whispers of the heart.

After all, there is a
part of you that knows
that having less can
mean living more.

There are no truer words, I have
had a lot in my life, lost a lot just the
same... always be honest with yourself,
who you are & what you want - you may
lose things. or people in the process, but
your happiness is priceless - always listen
to your heart.   ~ Nicci

"They can't stop talking about my transformation. But I can only do it once in my lifetime.

Do whatever makes YOU happy! Be a wonderful, adventurous, rad person for no one but YOU!! :)

-Shelby

No one can dictate what

ATTITUDE

you will wear today.
If you meet someone whose intent
is to put you down,
remember it is you
who wears the

CROWN.

Do not plant your dreams in the FIELD OF INDECISION, where nothing ever grows but the WEEDS OF "WHAT-IF."

To be at **peace**, your opinion of yourself must outweigh the assumptions of others about who you are.

It is a conscious decision that their words no longer have the ability to keep you down.

IF PEOPLE THINK YOU'RE AN ODDBALL AND DO NOT UNDERSTAND THE SOURCE OF YOUR HAPPINESS, KEEP ON SMILING. UNDER NO CIRCUMSTANCE, LET ANYONE DEFINE YOU!

How can you say sadness
overwhelms your night

SKY,

when I see a cluster of stars dancing in your

EYES?

All the puzzle pieces are in your hands!
Don't go looking for someone to complete it for you.
That only reinforces the fear you are incomplete.

Life's strongest glue is being happy to be you!

Growing old with someone else is

BEAUTIFUL,

but growing old while being true to yourself is

DIVINE.

THE SOUL DOES NOT ABSORB NEGATIVITY BY ACCIDENT, ONLY BY CHOICE.

KNOWING WHO YOU ARE IS THE BEST DEFENSE AGAINST WHO THEY THINK YOU ARE.

There are friendships imprinted in our

HEARTS

that will never be diminished by time and

DISTANCE.

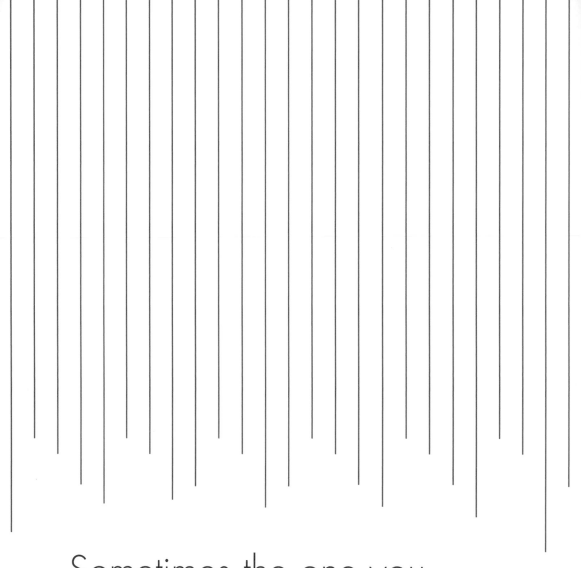

Sometimes the one you dismiss so easily is the one who will stay to weather the storm with you.

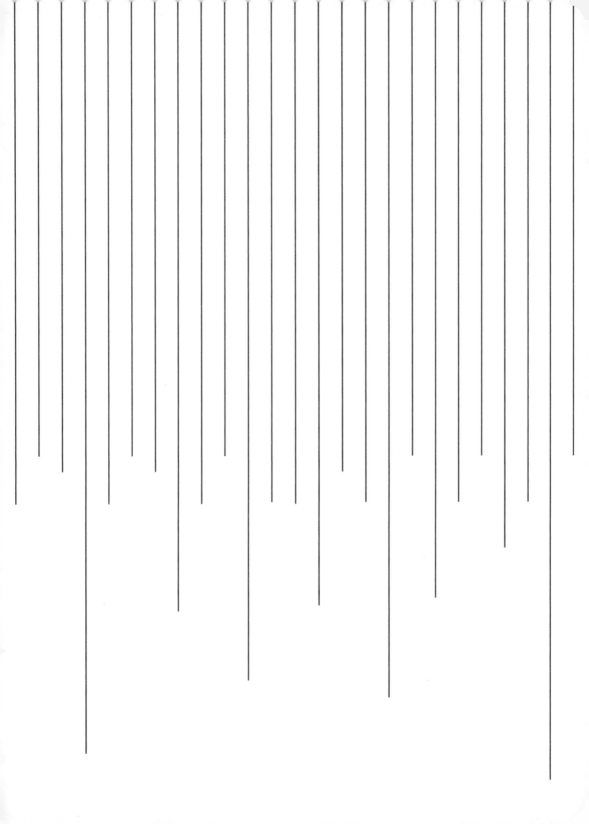

To strengthen the muscles of your

HEART,

the best exercise is lifting someone else's

SPIRIT

whenever you can.

You cannot avoid **bad days.** Sometimes you will shut a lot of doors, dimming your own **light** and creating a **mindset** of woefulness.

Although we are responsible for our own happiness, having a friend that opens more doors than you close is truly one of life's greatest blessings.

Do not worry about others
leaving you behind.
They are not going
where you are headed.

It is not who
finished first
but who saw the
most of life.

If you travel on a path that makes you happy and you are misunderstood by many, I hope you consider the opinion that carries the most weight—YOURS.

Kaylee,
These words are some of the truest I have ever read! I hope you make the life you want! We are here to help. Always—DAD

YOU CAN'T STOP
PEOPLE FROM
PASSING JUDGMENT.
BUT THEY CAN'T BUILD
YOUR PRISON—
YOU DO.

They who do not
fear darkness
have learned to
light their own candle.

I hope you know that who you truly are can

NEVER

be replaced by who they

IMAGINED

and wanted you to be.

Be grateful
to those who left you,
for their absence gave you
the strength to grow
in the space
they abandoned.

WHEN I REACH THE PLACE OF MY DREAMS, I WILL THANK MY FAILURES AND TEARS.

THEY, TOO, KEPT ME GOING.

Acknowledgments

To my parents, Melba N. and Rustico N., who raised me with love and asked nothing but for me to be the best person I could be. To my friends, Arthur G., Carolyn B., Tracy M. and Sandra K., who served as fuel to my dreams and asked nothing but for me to keep on shining. To my agent, Wendy K. and editors Shana D. and Deirdre B., who believed in me and made this dream a reality. To my readers, who continue to engage with me and share my writings with family and friends: You validate what I do. Thank you all!
—Dodinsky

About the Author

At an early age, Dodinksy searched for life's meaning

and came to see the world from a unique perspective.

He recognizes the simplicity in the most complex situations,

masterfully perceives the emotions involved, and from

these, weaves words that inspire people's spirits.

If you have enjoyed this book
or it has touched your life in some way,
we would love to hear from you.

Please send your comments to:
Hallmark Book Feedback
P.O. Box 419034
Mail Drop 100
Kansas City, MO 64141

Or e-mail us at:
booknotes@hallmark.com